THE NEW SYSTEM

OF

WRITTEN ACCENTUATION

PRESCRIBED BY THE

ROYAL ACADEMY OF SPAIN

BY

LIEUT. HENRY R. LEMLY, U.S.A.

AUTHOR OF "TÁCTICA DE INFANTERÍA," (UPTON), "EJERCICIOS GIMNÁSTICOS," "MANUAL OF STRATEGY" (FIX), ETC.

BOSTON, U.S.A.
GINN & COMPANY, PUBLISHERS
1890

Typography by J. S. Cushing & Co., Boston, U.S.A.

Presswork by Ginn & Co., Boston, U.S.A.

The existence of numerous and costly Spanish text-books, which are correct with the single exception of the accentuation, has suggested the preparation of this little pamphlet, embodying the latest rules upon the subject from the Spanish Royal Academy.

NEW SYSTEM

OF

WRITTEN ACCENTUATION.

I.

PRELIMINARY IDEAS.

1. Prosodical accent is the greater emphasis given a particular syllable of a word in pronunciation.

In Spanish, words are divided, according to the accented syllable, into *agudas*, *llanas*, and *esdrújulas*.

Agudas (or **Oxítonas**) are those which are accented upon the last syllable; as, *amó, están, venís, Tomé, Medellín, Santander,* etc.

Llanas (**Graves** or **Paroxítonas**) are those which are accented upon the penultimate syllable; as, *amo, vienen, resumen, amigo, concurrieron, Lucus,* etc.

Esdrújulas (or **Proparoxítonas**) are those which are accented upon the antepenultimate syllable; as, *límite, témese, jóvenes, generalísimo,* etc.

2. In Spanish, vowels are divided into *llenas* or *fuertes* (strong) and *débiles* (weak).

The former are *a, o, e.*

The latter, *i, u.*

3. The written accent (´), called *tilde,* serves to indicate the vowel which should be emphasized in pronunciation.

As it would be very inconvenient, in writing, to place this accent above all words, these have been grouped, by agreement, according to certain orthoepical laws, and the *tilde* is used to mark the exceptions.

For example: if the rule be that words are generally *llanas,* or perhaps *agudas,* the *esdrújulas* should be written with the accent, because exceptional.

The systems of written accentuation have varied according to the method of this grouping of words, adopted by different grammarians or preceptors.

The latest system by the Spanish Academy is the simplest and most logical of all.

4. The *tilde* or written accent is employed:

First, to indicate the accented syllable in those cases which are considered exceptions, as, for example, in *místico* (because *esdrújula,* and hence of exceptional pronunciation); in *borceguí, leyó* (because the greater number of words terminating in a vowel are *llanas*); in *dócil, Híjar* (because nearly all words terminating in a consonant, other than *n* or *s*, are usually *llanas*).

Second, to indicate the dissolution of concurrent vowels. *Saúco,* whether accented upon the *u* or the *a,* is *llana;* so likewise are *tenia, venia* (nouns), and *tenía, venía* (verbs). Therefore, as stated above, in neither case should the accent be written, because words ending in vowels are generally *llanas.* However, the nouns *tenia* and *venia* are not accented; while the verbs *tenía* and *venía* are, as well as the substantives *saúco, egoísmo,* etc., in order to show that the vowels in question do not form diphthongs, and the accent is placed above the weak vowel.

Third, to distinguish words, otherwise identical in structure, as *dé*, verb, and *de*, preposition; or in one of which the accent is strong and emphatic, while weak in the other, as *sóbre*, verb, and *sobre*, preposition; *vén*, imperative, and *ven* indicative. This is the diacritical accent (*acento diacrítico*).

Fourth, to separate the particles *á*, *é*, *ó*, *ú*, which, although without the prosodical accent in pronunciation, bear the *tilde*, in order that they may stand apart to the sight (especially in manuscript), and not be confounded with the preceding or following word.

Let us now extract from the last edition of the grammar of the Academy the orthoepical principles from which are derived the exceptions that, in turn, are converted into orthographical rules.

II.

ORTHOEPICAL LAWS.

Terminations in n. — The syllables *an, en, on* — the vowel unaccented — terminate the third person plural in eleven tenses of the verb, varied into seventeen forms; from which we deduce, multiplying said number by eight thousand verbs, that there are a great many *llanas* of this class in the Spanish language; as, *aman, tenían, partieron, hablen, creyeran, sentirían, contemplasen, olvidasen*, etc.

The third person plural of the future tense of the indicative mood, which is *aguda*, is an exception; as, *amarán, partirán*, etc.

With respect to the remaining words which terminate in *n*, the number of which is greatly inferior to that of the verbs, the opposite obtains, that is, the most of them are *agudas;* as: *alquitrán, baladrán, zaratán; sartén, también, vaivén; motín, espadín, Albaicín; almidón, barracón, Cicerón, formaeión, razón, sermón; atún, ningún, según*, etc.

The following are *graves* or *llanas: alguien, Arizcun, Carmen, chirumen, dolmen, Esteben, germen, imagen, joven, margen, orden, origen, resumen, virgen*, etc. And *esdrújula-régimen.*

Many identical words terminate in *n*, which are only distinguished from each other by the accent; as:

aman	Amán	borren	borrén	hacen	Hacén
amen	amén	caen	Caén	oran	Orán
anden	andén	casaron	casarón	pasaron	Pasarón
aran	Arán	cascaron	cascarón	picaron	picarón
Baden	Badén	colon	Colón	salen	Salén
bailen	Bailén	duran	Durán	sellen	Sellén
batan	batán	escoben	escobén	etc.,	etc.

Terminations in s. — The greater number of words terminating in *s* are *llanas,* and they greatly exceed those ending in *n,* inasmuch as the former letter is the distinctive termination of the plural of all nouns, as well as of different persons in all the tenses of the verb. For example: *arpas, letras, vidas, coronas, frutas; doradas, excelsas, temidas, honrosas, muchas; amemos, temas, partieres; Ceres, Paris* (the Trojan), *Adonis,* etc.

The following are exceptions, because *agudas:* the second person plural of the present of the indicative; the second persons, singular and plural, of the future indicative; and the second person plural of the present subjunctive: *averiguáis, averiguarás, averiguaréis, averigüéis,* etc.

Also, for the same reason, other words, not verbs, as *además, jamás, ciprés, pavés,* and the national names *alavés, calabrés, portugués,* etc.; *anís, chisgaravís, maravedís, semidiós, obús, Caifás, Andrés, Amadís, Beltenebrós, Emaús,* etc.

The following are exceptions, because *esdrújulas:* the first person plural of the imperfect indicative, and the imperfect and future subjunctive: *amábamos; temiéramos, temeríamos,* and *temiésemos; partiéremos,* etc.

There are many identical words terminating in *s,*

which, as before explained for those ending in *n*, are only distinguished from each other by the accent; as:

alas	Alás	cortes	cortés	montes	montés
aulas	Aulás	delfines	delfinés	ojos	Ojós
amos	Amós	fines	finés	Paris	París
anas	Anás	gines	Ginés	selles	Sellés
ares	Arés	girones	gironés	tomas	Tomás
arras	Arrás	leones	leonés	valles	Vallés
banastas	Banastás	marques	marqués	veras	verás
berros	Berrós	meras	Merás	etc., etc.	
Borbones	Borbonés	monas	monás		

Nouns and adjectives, when their number is modified, usually suffer a corresponding change of accent.

Those ending in a vowel, if *llanas*, do not vary the accent upon forming the plural; as:

mano	manos	firme	firmes
roca	rocas	dura	duras

If they end in a consonant, they become *esdrújulas* in the plural; as:

cráter	cráteres	germen	gérmenes	dúctil	dúctiles
flébil	flébiles	virgen	vírgenes	útil	útiles

(An exception is *carácter*, the plural of which, to-day, is *caracteres*.)

If *agudas*, whether terminating in a vowel or consonant, they become *llanas* in the plural; as:

alelí	alelíes	guardian	guardianes	atroz	atroces
astur	astures	carmesí	carmesíes	infiel	infieles
bajá	bajaes	marcial	marciales	etc., etc.	

III.

ORTHOGRAPHICAL RULES.

Words of more than one syllable, terminating in a vowel, if *agudas*, require the written accent.

If they end in a consonant other than *n* or *s*, they are not thus accented, as *Godoy*. The final *y*, although sounded like a vowel, is considered a consonant for the purposes of accentuation.

Those ending in *n* or *s* must be accented ; as, *alacrán*, *andén*, *espadín*, *corazón*, *atún*, *amarán*, *temerán*, *partirán*, *también*, *ningún*, *según* ; *Amán*, *Durán*, *Bailén*, *Albaicín*, *Cicerón*, *Sahagún* ; *compás*, *revés*, *anís*, *semidiós*, *patatús* ; *verás*, *prevés*, *compartís* ; *además*, *atrás*, *jamás* ; *Barabás*, *Moisés*, *París* (city), *Ojós*, *Portús*, etc.

Words terminating in a vowel, if *llanas*, are not accented. If they end in a consonant, they are accented, unless it be *n* or *s*, in which case they are not accented ; as, *virgen*, *volumen* ; *aman*, *bailen*, *duran*, *pensaron*, *vienen*, *conocieron* ; *Tasman*, *Carmen*, *Yemer*, *Oyarzun* ; *martes*, *jueves*, *sintaxis*, *crisis*, *dosis*, *virus*, *campanas*, *veras*, *diamantes*, *ojos* ; *adoras*, *vences*, *huyes*, *amaras*, *temieras*, *partieres*, *amaremos* ; *Lucas*, *Cervantes*, *Paris* (the Trojan), *Carlos*, *Nicodemus*, etc.

Words terminating in two vowels, when *llanas*, must be accented if the first vowel is weak and receives the emphasis in pronunciation, whether or not followed by final *n* or *s* ; as, *poesía*, *desvarío*, *falúa*, *dúo*, *tenía*, *sería, Darío, Benalúa, Ríu, Espelúy, Túy*[1]; *desvaríos,* etc.; *tenían, considerarías,* etc.; *Isaías, Jermías, Darnius,* etc.

In *agudas,* containing a strong vowel combined with a weak, accented one, the latter should bear the *tilde;* as, *país, raís, ataúd, baúl, Saúl,* etc.

An accented, weak vowel, followed by a diphthong and final *s,* as in certain persons of the verb, should likewise bear the *tilde;* as, *teníais, decíais,* etc.

But *llanas* which end in a diphthong, or in two strong vowels, whether followed or not by a final *n* or *s,* obey the general rule, and are not accented: *patria, tenia* (tape-worm), *seria, delirio, sitio, agua, fatuo; acaricia, atestigua; bacalao, deseo, canoa, corroe, Galisteo, Bidasoa; albricias, patrias, fatuos, lidian, amortiguan, trataseis, leyereis, Clinias, Titaguas, Esquivias; bacalaos, canoas, corroen,* etc.

If there is a diphthong in the syllable of a word — *aguda, llana,* or *esdrújula* — which, according to the rules prescribed, should be accented, the *tilde* must be placed above the strong vowel, or if both are weak, over the second; as, *buscapié, acaricié, parabién, veréis, después; Rupiá, Sebastián, Navasqués, benjuí, jaragüí; guájar, Huércal, Liétor; piélago, Cáucaso,* etc.

Monosyllabic verbs with diphthongs follow the same rule; as, *fué, fuí, dió, vió,* etc.

The adverb *aun,* when it precedes the verb or part of speech which it modifies, is not accented, because, in this case, the two vowels form a diphthong; but when

[1] In these two words the *tilde* is placed above the *u,* because, according to the Academy, there is no diphthong. *Cocuy, muy,* are not accented, because in these words the *u* and *y* form a diphthong.

it follows said word, it should be accented, as it is then pronounced like a dissyllabic *aguda;* as *¿ Aun no han venido ? — No han venido aún.*

The triphthong is accented upon the strong vowel; as, *amortiguáis, despreciéis,* etc.

Latin words, or those of other languages employed in Spanish, and foreign proper names, are accented, as far as possible, in accordance with the rules already prescribed for Spanish words; as, *ítem, memorándum, execuátur, tránseat, Schlégel, Wínckelmann, Tolón, Windsor,* etc.

In accordance with the foregoing rules, *héroe, erróneo, Dánae, hectárea, flúido,* and similar words, are accented, because they are *esdrújulas;* the second person singular of the verb, *amáis, teméis, amaréis, temeréis, améis, temáis,* etc., because *agudas* terminating in *s*; the verbal forms, *decía, decían,* etc., because combinations in which the weak and not the strong vowel bears the accent (see recent publications by the Spanish Academy); likewise the plurals, as *días míos, mías, tías, países, baúles, paraísos,* etc.; the participles, as *raído, roído, creído,* and such words as *egoísmo, egoísta, saúco, creíble, aúlla,* etc.

Applying the rules cited above, *agudas* of more than one syllable, terminating in *n* or *s*, as *León, Jaén, jamás, revés, partís, Jesús,* etc., should be accented; but not monosyllables of like termination, as *Juan, buen, bien, cien, fin, pan, Dios, Luis, pues,* nor *estoico, heroico, deseo, Baena, ruina, viuda, ruido* (Grammar of the Academy, page 364), because the latter are *llanas,* and end in a vowel. However, words like *continúo, gradúe,* etc., are accented, because, although *llanas* and terminating in a vowel, they possess the same characteristics if pronounced *continuo*, *gradue*, with the accent upon the *i* and *a*.

The diacritical accent is indispensable for distinguishing words of the same form but different meaning; as:

amamos (present),	*amámos* (preterit).
batimos (present),	*batímos* (preterit).
luego (conjunction),	*luégo* (adverb of time).
solo (adjective),	*sólo* (adverb).
mas (conjunction),	*más* (adjective or adverb).
son (verb),	*són* (substantive).
ve (present of *ver*),	*vé* (imperative of *ir*).
bajo (adjective and preposition),	*bájo* (verb).
si (conditional),	*sí* (pronoun or affirmative).
se (pronoun),	*sé* (verb).
de (preposition),	*dé* (verb).
quien (relative),	*quién* (interrogative).
etc.	etc.

RECAPITULATION.

For greater clearness the foregoing rules are reduced to the two following:

1. The *tilde* or written accent must be employed with—

All *agudas* of more than one syllable, terminating in a vowel or in *n* or *s*; as, *amé, oí, ambigú, ahí,* etc.; *panteón, jardín, tapón, están, interés, herís, podéis, oís, amáis,* etc.

All *graves* or *llanas,* terminating in a consonant other than *n* or *s*; as, *áspid, ángel, prócer,* etc.

All *esdrújulas* and *sobresdrújulas;* as, *héroe, flúido, amásemos, cedíamos, jóvenes, castíguesemele, diríamostelo,* etc.

All words in which a strong and weak vowel concur, the latter being accented, in order to indicate the dissolution of the diphthong; as, *Caín, baúl, baúles, día, días, mío, míos, lío, guía, píe* (from *piar*), *aíra, bahía, creíble, egoísmo, continúo, extenúe, auxilío, oír,* etc.; and

All words which require it to distinguish them from others of like structure.

2. The *tilde* or written accent is omitted with all other classes of words; as, *vi, di* (from *dar*), *pie* (noun), *fe, Juan, bien, buen, Dios, Luis, res, mies, pies, dosel, placer, construido, tenue, restaura, auxilio, hay, convoy, muy, margen, Carmen, Carlos, Lucas,* etc.

www.ingramcontent.com/pod-product-compliance
Lightning Source LLC
LaVergne TN
LVHW010833120826
845149LV00016B/1368

* 9 7 8 1 4 1 8 1 9 0 4 7 7 *